# The Ultimate Self-Teaching Met...

# Play Piano Today!

## A Complete Guide to the Basics

by Sharon Stosur
Audio Arrangements by Peter Deneff
Produced by David Vartanian

**PLAYBACK+**
Speed • Pitch • Balance • Loop

To access audio and video visit:
**www.halleonard.com/mylibrary**

Enter Code
7004-0716-6890-4164

ISBN 978-1-5400-5234-6

Visit Hal Leonard Online at
**www.halleonard.com**

Contact us:
**Hal Leonard**
7777 West Bluemound Road
Milwaukee, WI 53213
Email: info@halleonard.com

In Europe, contact:
**Hal Leonard Europe Limited**
42 Wigmore Street
Marylebone, London, W1U 2RN
Email: info@halleonardeurope.com

In Australia, contact:
**Hal Leonard Australia Pty. Ltd.**
4 Lentara Court
Cheltenham, Victoria, 3192 Australia
Email: info@halleonard.com.au

# Contents

# Introduction

Track 1

Welcome to *Play Piano Today!*, the series designed to teach you the basics of playing the piano. Whether you've had some music experience, or you're an absolute beginner, *Play Piano Today!* will have you playing tunes and making music right away!

Track 2

# About the Audio & Video

It's easy and fun to play the piano, and the accompanying audio will make learning even more enjoyable as we take you step by step through each lesson and play each song along with a full band. Much like with a traditional lesson, the best way to learn this material is to read and practice a while first on your own, and then listen to the audio. *Play Piano Today!* is designed to allow you to learn at your own pace. If there is ever something that you don't quite understand the first time through, go back to the audio and listen again. Use the Playback+ feature online to adjust the tempo as you learn each song. Every musical track has been given a track number, so when you want to practice a song again, you can find it right away.

Some topics in the book include video lessons, so you can see and hear the material being taught. Audio and video are indicated with icons.

 Audio Icon      Video Icon

# The Basics

Track 3

## Posture

Good posture at the piano makes everything easier! The bench should face the keyboard squarely. Sit up straight with your arms hanging loosely from your shoulders. You'll know if your bench is at a proper height if your elbows are slightly higher than the keyboard.

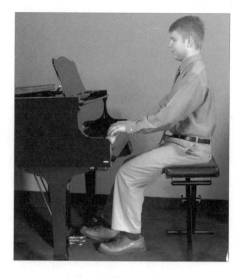

Track 4

## Right Hand and Left Hand

When playing the piano your fingers are numbered 1-5, with the thumb as number 1.

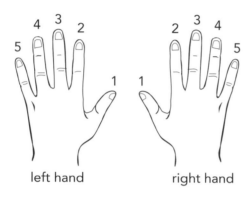

left hand          right hand

Track 5

As you play the keys, keep your fingers curved and the knuckles of your hands rounded, not flat. A rounded hand position will help your fingers move more freely.

Track 6

## The Keyboard

The keyboard is organized in groups of black and white keys. The black keys are easy to see in groups of two and three.

The white keys are named using the first seven letters of the alphabet: **A B C D E F G**

C is always to the left of the group of 2 black keys:

F is always to the left of the group of 3 black keys:

On a full-size piano there are 88 keys: 52 white keys and 36 black keys. The lowest white key is A. The eight note, white-key pattern A-B-C-D-E-F-G repeats over and over, from low to high. The C nearest the middle of the keyboard is called **Middle C**.

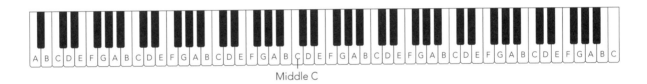

Middle C

Take some time to learn the names of the white keys. One way to do this is to use the black keys as a guide, and play the white keys in groups, CDE, from low to high, and backward from high to low. Repeat this with FGAB.

Another way to practice is to play all the white keys from the lowest to highest, and then backward, high to low. If you forget the name of a white key, just refer to one of the diagrams here. Soon you'll have them memorized!

# Playing the White Keys

Here's the beginning of a familiar tune, "Jingle Bells." Use your right hand to play the white keys. The letters indicate which keys to play. The numbers above the letters indicate which fingers to use. Continue figuring out the rest of the notes using your ear. Don't be afraid to experiment a little. Sing along if you like.

| 3 | 3 | 3 | | 3 | 3 | 3 | | 3 | 5 | 1 | 2 | 3 |
|---|---|---|---|---|---|---|---|---|---|---|---|---|
| E | E | E ____ | | E | E | E ____ | | E | G | C | D | E ____ |
| Jin - | gle | bells, ___ | | jin - | gle | bells, ___ | | jin - | gle | all | the | way. _____ |

# Reading Music

At the piano, usually the right hand plays the melody. That's where we'll start learning some of the fundamentals of music that will get you moving around the keys in no time!

## Notes

Track 7

Music is written with symbols called *notes*. Each type of note has a specific rhythmic value. Often a quarter note is used to represent one beat. All other rhythmic values are determined in relationship to the note that gets one beat.

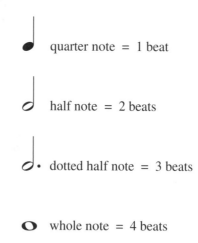

quarter note = 1 beat

half note = 2 beats

dotted half note = 3 beats

whole note = 4 beats

## Staff

Track 8

Notes are placed on a *staff*; five horizontal lines and four spaces. Placement of these notes on the staff determines *pitch*, how high or low a note will sound. The higher the note is placed on the staff, the higher it will sound; the lower the note is placed on the staff, the lower it will sound. Since not all notes will fit on just five lines and four spaces, *ledger lines* are used to extend the staff.

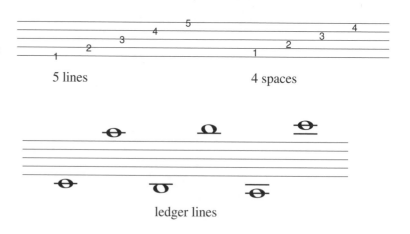

5 lines                    4 spaces

ledger lines

## Clef

Track 9

A symbol called a *clef* indicates where the notes will be played on the keyboard. The right hand will play notes written in the *treble* clef. Here's an easy way to remember the names of the treble clef notes.

E   G   B   D   F

(**E**very **G**ood **B**oy **D**oes **F**ine)

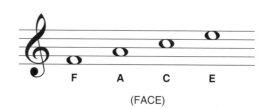

F   A   C   E

(FACE)

# Rhythm

Track 10

To organize the notes on the staff into *measures*, *bar lines* are used. A *time signature* determines how many beats will be in each measure. The top number of the time signature indicates the number of beats per measure, and the bottom number names the note that gets one beat.

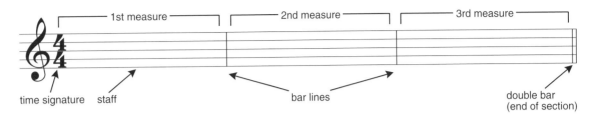

Remember the first line of "Jingle Bells" from the previous lesson? Here's how it would look in music notation, written on the staff.

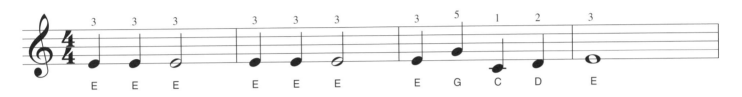

# Jingle Bells

Track 11

You're ready to play the whole tune now. Use your right hand, placing your thumb on Middle C. Find Middle C by locating the C that is in the middle range of the keyboard.

Words and Music by J. Pierpont

Remember, you can adjust the tempo of the audio accompaniment, playing slowly at first, and increasing the tempo as you wish.

7

# The Right Hand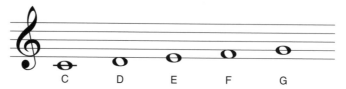

Let's continue to work with the right hand playing the melody. Once you're comfortable with the right hand, it will be easy to add the left hand, and get both hands playing together.

## C Position

Track 12

Five consecutive notes in a row on the keyboard can sometimes be referred to as a *position*. For example, when you place your five fingers on C-D-E-F-G, you are playing in the *C position*. Since most songs have more than five notes, the position acts like a home base, or starting point, for your hand.

Track 13

You're ready to play this famous theme from Beethoven's Fifth Symphony. This tune uses just five notes, C-D-E-F-G in the C position. Place your right-hand thumb on Middle C, and your consecutive fingers on the notes that follow. Remember, Middle C is in the middle of the keyboard. Notice whether the notes repeat, move up, or move down. When notes move up or down, one to the next, we describe the music as moving in *steps*.

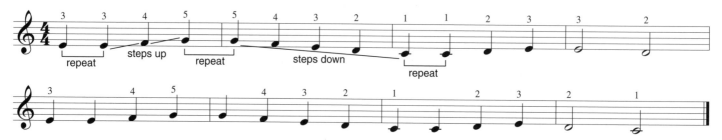

## Music Review

Before you play "When the Saints Go Marching In," let's take a few minutes to review some of the music fundamentals we learned in Lesson 2.

First, notice the time signature. The number four on top means there are four beats per measure. The number four on the bottom means the quarter note gets one beat. Three different types of notes make up this song, quarter notes, half notes, and whole notes. The rhythmic values are below:

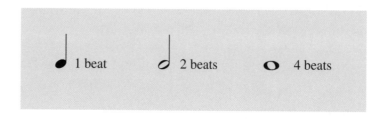

# Rests

You'll also see some new symbols, *quarter rests* and *half rests*. Rests have their own rhythmic value, corresponding to the notes with the same name. Rests are symbols for *silence* in music, or when you **don't** play.

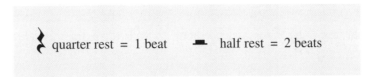

quarter rest = 1 beat     half rest = 2 beats

# Steps and Skips

There are lots of notes that move by step in "When the Saints," and there are also notes that *skip*, that is, when a note moves from a line to a line, or a space to a space, *skipping* a note on both the staff and keyboard.

"When the Saints" is played in the C Position. Place your right-hand thumb on Middle C before you begin. Finger numbers are given to guide you. Play at a slow *tempo* (speed) the first time, looking for notes that step, skip, or repeat. Then play at a faster tempo, and sing along if you like!

Track 14

# When the Saints Go Marching In

Words by Katherine E. Purvis
Music by James M. Black

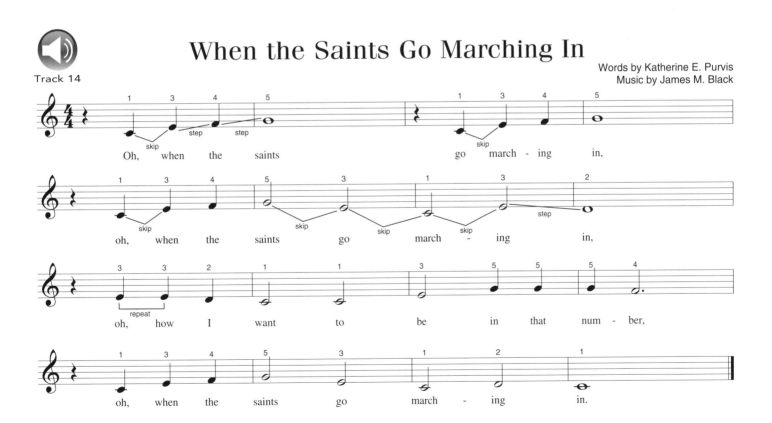

# Ties

Here's another song written with the five notes of the C Position. "Beautiful Brown Eyes" is a traditional folk song with a slow and easy feel. Note the tempo marking, *Gently*, above the time signature. The quarter note still gets one beat, and there are three beats per measure.

This song gives us a chance to learn a new symbol. Notice the long curved line connecting the half notes in measures three and four. This is a *tie*. A tie is used to extend the length of a note across a bar line. Play the F, and continue to hold the F for the value of the second half note, without re-playing it. Now that first F will be held for a total of four beats. Two beats for the first half note, and two more beats for the tied half note.

There's another tie in measures seven and eight. The dotted half note is held for three beats, plus one more beat, because it's tied to a quarter note in the next measure.

As you get ready to play "Beautiful Brown Eyes," scan through the song looking for repeated notes, steps, and skips. You'll notice two places where there is a slightly larger skip, a G down to a D. This is very easy to play, especially when you're looking ahead and ready for it. We've included fingering here to help.

# Analyzing a Piece of Music

Music can be organized in many ways. Sometimes this can be as simple as one musical idea, like the song you just learned, "When the Saints Go Marching In." Other times a song can have two musical ideas that alternate, like a verse and chorus, and longer, more complicated tunes can be composed using several musical ideas.

"Beautiful Brown Eyes" is twice as long as "When the Saints." Let's take a closer look at the *form* of this tune, or, in other words, how it was composed. This traditional folk song has two sections of four lines each, with a slight change in the repeated section.

Look through the first four lines, playing the notes and singing the lyrics. You may have noticed that line one and line three are exactly the same. Lines two and four are different. Knowing this helps you learn the song more quickly.

Now compare the second four lines of the song with the first four lines. What do you notice? The second half of the song is almost exactly like the first half, with the exception of line six, which differs a bit from line two.

One way to learn this song would be to focus on the first four lines, then jump ahead to learn line six. Now you can play the whole song from the beginning, because you've learned all the parts.

# Beautiful Brown Eyes

Right Hand:

Traditional

**Gently**

Wil - lie, oh, Wil - lie, I love you, _____

love you with all _____ my heart. _____ To -

mor - row we might have been mar - ried, _____ but

drink - in' has kept us a - part. _____

Beau - ti - ful, beau - ti - ful brown eyes, _____

beau - ti - ful, beau - ti - ful brown eyes. _____

Beau - ti - ful, beau - ti - ful brown eyes, _____ I'll

nev - er love blue eyes a - gain. _____

# Adding the Left Hand

When the right hand plays the melody, the left hand can play *harmony*. This often takes the form of *chords*, three or more notes played at the same time. Using your left hand to add chords to a melody is an easy way to create a full sound at the piano.

## C Position for Left Hand

Track 17

Find the C eight notes lower than Middle C, moving left down the keyboard from Middle C until you get to the next lower C. Instead of placing your thumb on the C, place your fifth finger on the C, as shown below.

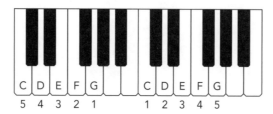

Practice playing the five notes, C-D-E-F-G moving up and down a few times, to get the feel for your left hand on the keys. If you are right-handed, playing the keys with your left hand may feel a bit awkward, but after a few minutes or so you should be feeling quite warmed-up!

## C and G Chords

Track 18

A *chord* is three or more notes played at the same time. You can play a chord starting on any note. To play a C chord with your left hand, place your hand in C position, below Middle C. Play the notes C, E, and G at the same time, to sound the C chord. It might take a few tries to play all three notes together, but as you continue to work at it, those notes will come together easily.

To play a G chord, keep your left hand in the same place on the keyboard. You'll need the notes G, B, and D to play a G chord. Move to the G chord *from* the C chord. The two chords have one note in common: G. Keep your thumb on G, and move finger 3 down to the D, and finger 5 down to the B. Play the G chord, B-D-G from bottom to top. Practice moving from the C chord to the G chord and back again, until this feels easy and comfortable.

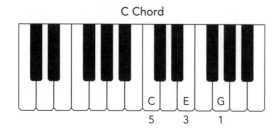

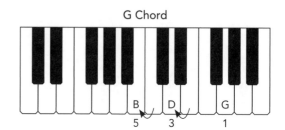

12

# Lead Sheet Notation

There are several ways to notate and play the left-hand part in piano music. We'll use a *lead sheet*. This type of notation includes the melody written in the treble clef for the right hand to play, and single letters above the treble staff that represent chords the left hand will play.

Take a look at "Ode to Joy," a song you are familiar with from the last lesson. There is a letter above the first note of each measure. This names the chord your left hand will play. Play the chord with your left hand on the first beat of each measure, and *sustain* the chord (holding it down), for the entire measure. Continue to play the left-hand chords on the first beat of each measure as indicated. Before you begin, take a minute to carefully place each hand in the C position.

## Ode to Joy

By Ludwig van Beethoven

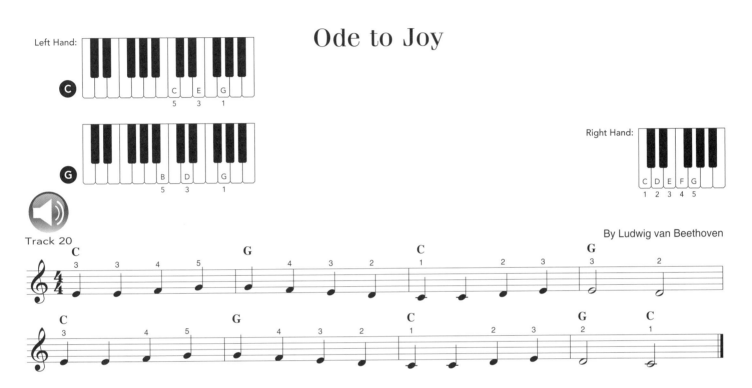

Here's another folk song using the C and G chords. Play through the melody to familiarize yourself with the tune. Place your left hand in the C position, and practice moving from the C to the G chords. There are two measures where the left hand will play the G chord. Take note of where those places are before you begin to play.

## Go Tell Aunt Rhody

Traditional

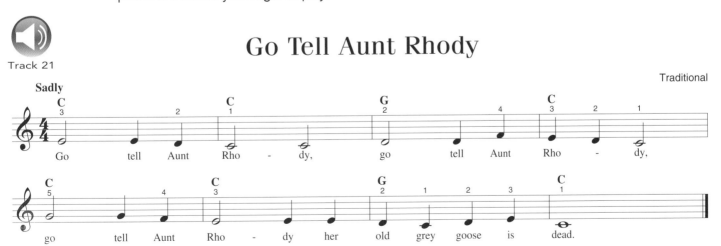

Track 22

# Moving away from the C Position

As you know, most songs are written using more than five notes. Starting in C position, the right-hand thumb can stretch down to play additional lower notes, or the fifth finger can stretch up to play higher notes. Take a look at "Marianne," below. I've marked the places where the thumb moves down one note to play the B in the melody.

# Tempo and Dynamics

Track 23

You'll also notice a *tempo* marking right above the time signature. This gives you information about the speed and mood of the song. *Dynamics* indicate how soft or loud the song will be. Dynamics are usually written with symbols for the Italian words they represent. Play this song *mf*, *mezzo forte*, which means medium loud.

$f$ (forte) loud

$p$ (piano) soft

$mf$ (mezzo forte) medium loud

$mp$ (mezzo piano) medium soft

Track 24

# Marianne

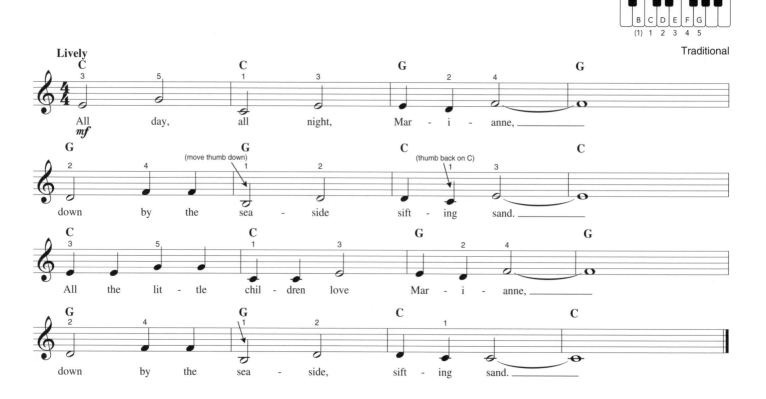

14

# More Notes and a New Chord

## The F Chord

Track 25

Now that you know how to play C and G chords, you can add another chord. The F chord uses the notes F, A and C. Starting with your left hand playing a C chord, move your thumb up to play A, use finger 2 to play F, and keep finger 5 on the C. Study the diagram below and practice moving from the C chord to the F chord until you feel comfortable.

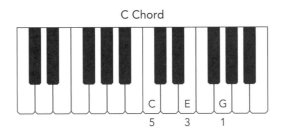

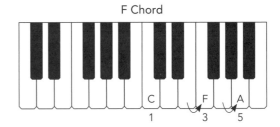

## Have Some Fun with the Saints

You played the melody for "When the Saints Go Marching In" back in Lesson 3. Now you can add the left-hand chords. Play through the chord changes, and you'll notice the F chord in measures 12-13, and the quick chord change, C-G-C, in the last two measures. There is no dynamic marking at the beginning of the song. Decide how you would like to play this song, and write in your own dynamics.

Track 26

## When the Saints Go Marching In

Words by Katherine E. Purvis
Music by James M. Black

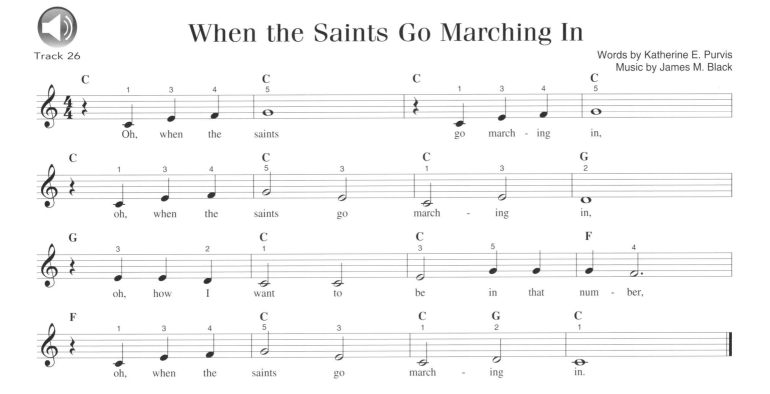

# An Elvis Presley Classic

You might recognize this next tune as "Love Me Tender," sung by Elvis Presley. His popular hit is based on this American folk song.

The first time through "Aura Lee," play with your right hand alone. This gives you a chance to hear the tune and double check any notes you're unsure about. Notice that in the next-to-last measure finger 5 stretches up to play the A. Now, add the left-hand chords written above the staff. Remember, both hands will be playing in the C position.

## Aura Lee

Words by W.W. Fosdick
Music by George R. Poulton

Track 27

Take a look at the fingering provided in "Kum Bah Yah." In order for the fifth finger to stretch up one note to play the A in measure two, play the E with finger 2 and the G with finger 4. Try the right hand alone once to get a feel for this. As you learn more songs you'll learn to stretch and move your hand as needed to get around the keyboard. Take note of the fingering given, and if you're unsure of a note name, refer back to earlier lessons. Don't be afraid to let your ear help you out. Singing as you play can often lead you to the correct notes!

Track 28

## Kum Bah Yah

Traditional Spiritual

Track 29

# Pick-up Notes

Sometimes an incomplete measure begins a piece of music. The notes that appear before the first full measure are called *pick-up notes*. Although they represent only a partial measure, they are still counted in the same way. Often the beats that are missing from this incomplete measure are accounted for in the very last measure of the piece, as they are in both "Kum Bah Yah" and "Oh, Susannah."

# Repeat Sign

A double bar with two dots is a musical symbol called a *repeat sign*, and indicates to repeat a section, or entire piece of music.

# Stretching Beyond the C Position

The melody in "Oh, Susannah" stretches up to A. Follow the fingering given to do this easily. Notice the repeat sign in measure eight. Go back to the repeat sign at the first full measure of the song and continue.

## Oh, Susannah

# 1st and 2nd Endings

Track 32

When brackets accompany the repeat sign, you have *1st and 2nd endings*. Take a look at the 1st and 2nd ending brackets at the end of "Michael, Row the Boat Ashore." The first time, play the measure marked with bracket number 1. Go back to the repeat sign, and this time, skip the first bracket and play the measure marked with bracket number 2. 1st and 2nd endings are often used when there is more than one verse in a song.

Notice the fingering in "Michael, Row the Boat Ashore." Your right hand starts with thumb on Middle C. Finger 2 stretches to play the E. This allows you to play A with finger 5 in the following measure. At the beginning of the second line, finger 5 moves to the G. This allows the thumb to play Middle C again in later measures.

Track 33

## Michael Row the Boat Ashore

Traditional Folksong

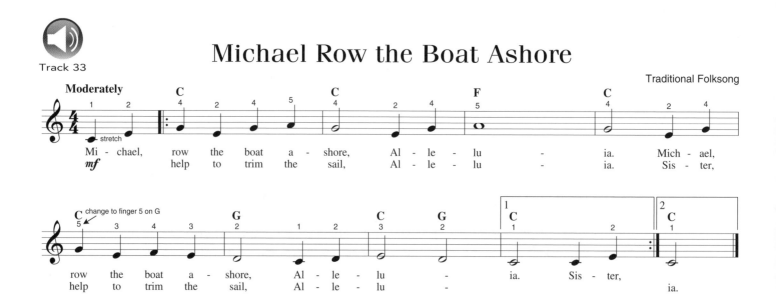

## Double the Fun!

Once you've learned the melody and chords, feel free to add more to the song. For example, in "Michael, Row the Boat Ashore," most of the measures have only one chord per measure in the left hand. Try repeating the chord, so there are now two chords per measure playing the chords on beats 1 and 3. You could also experiment with adding chords on each beat playing four chords per measure. Try new things with your right hand too. Some ideas might be playing higher or lower on the keyboard, or adding more notes to the melody. Consider using ideas from the accompaniment tracks, and feel free to create ideas of your own!

# Lesson 6 Eighth Notes

A quarter note can be divided in half. Two *eighth notes* equal one quarter note.

$$♪ + ♪ = ♩$$

A single eighth note looks like a quarter note with a flag. They are often beamed together to make them easier to read.

$$♪ + ♪ = \text{♫} = \text{1 beat}$$

$$♪ + ♪ + ♪ + ♪ = \text{♫♫} = \text{2 beats}$$

To count eighth notes, divide the quarter note and use "and" between the beats.

```
1   &   2   &   3  (&)  4  (&)
```

The French folk song "Frère Jacques" is often sung as a round. Sing and play through this simple melody to feel the change between quarter and eighth notes. When this rhythm feels easy, add the left-hand chords.

## Frère Jacques
### (Are You Sleeping)

Track 34

Traditional

19

# More Notes for Right Hand

So far we've been focusing on the notes near the lower end of the treble clef, and the ledger line middle C. Let's expand from there, to play notes on all five lines of the staff. Review the line and space notes below.

Did you know that the treble clef is also called the *G clef*? This is because the clef sign curls around the second line, designating that line as G.

This G is the G five notes higher than middle C. "Amazing Grace" begins with the right-hand thumb on this treble clef G.

In order to move around the keyboard easily, fingering is given to show when to stretch to notes and when to change fingers or positions. At first, reading the notes and finger numbers can be confusing, especially when you must move your hand to reach the next note. Take it slow the first few times, checking to be sure you're reading the correct note names, and use your ear, singing along as you play. When there are a lot of fingering shifts and changes it's a good idea to focus on the right hand first, and add the left-hand chords after you're comfortable playing the right-hand melody.

Track 35

## Amazing Grace

Words by John Newton
Traditional American Melody

## Stretching an Octave

This beautiful English folksong is written over an *octave*, eight notes from the treble clef G all the way up to the G just above the staff. In order for the right hand to play these notes easily, your fingers will move and stretch as needed. Use the fingering provided, and this will soon feel quite easy to do.

Track 36

## The Water Is Wide

Traditional

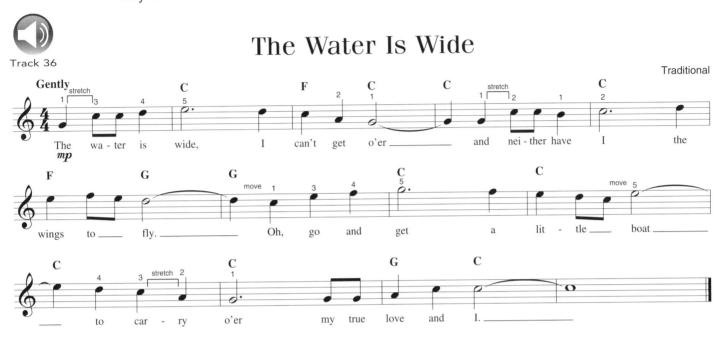

## Syncopation

The tied eighth notes in "Frankie and Johnny" create *syncopation*, a feeling of accent on a weak beat. Count the eighth notes using "and" to get the jazzy feel of the tied notes.

Track 37

## Frankie and Johnny

Anonymous Blues Ballad

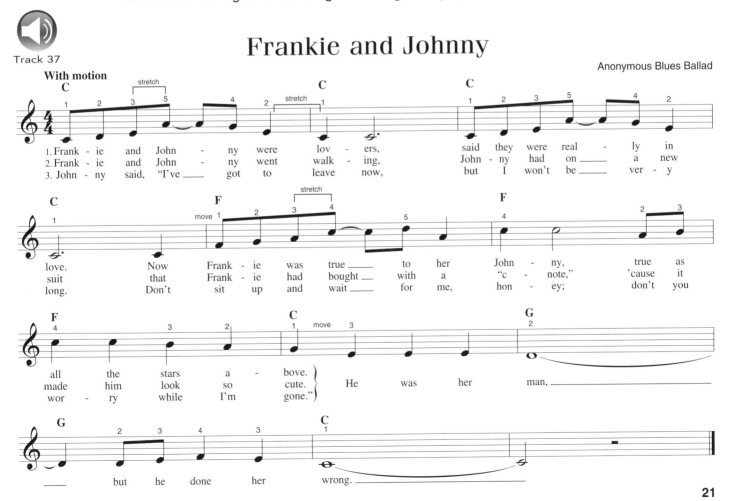

# Minor Chords and Accidentals

## Minor Chords

Track 38

Chords can have different qualities of sound; the most common are *major* and *minor*. The chords we've learned so far are major. C, F, and G have a bright quality that is easily recognized as major. Minor chords sound quite different. They have a darker, denser quality. Minor chords are always notated with a lower case **m** next to the letter name.

When you play D-F-A you have a D minor chord, notated as Dm. Play this chord with your left hand.

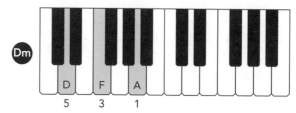

Now play the C major chord, followed by the Dm chord. Both use three white keys, but have very different sound qualities.

## Moving from Chord to Chord

"All Through the Night" includes a Dm chord in the left hand. You'll want to spend some time getting a feel for moving to and from this new chord.

Play through the left-hand chords. You'll notice that the Dm chord follows the F chord in this song. This makes it easy to play. Keep playing the F and A, and simply move your 5th finger up one key to play the D. There's your Dm chord!

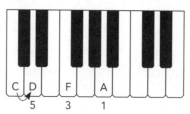

It's a bit trickier to get to the G chord from the Dm, but that G chord is so familiar to you now you'll pick this up in no time. From the Dm chord, stretch your 5th finger down to the B. Shift down to add the D and G, and you are back to the G chord. This pattern (also known as a *chord progression*) appears two more times, in lines 2 and 4. Keep working with your left hand alone until these chords feel easy and comfortable to play.

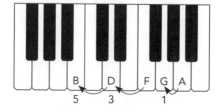

Let's add the left-hand chords to the beautiful Welsh folksong "All Through the Night." Take a look at line three to notice that your right hand will move up to the high F, the top line of the staff. Playing up in steps you'll reach a new ledger line note, high A. Stick to the fingering given to navigate your way back down the staff.

# All Through the Night

Welsh Folksong

Slowly

Sleep, my child, and peace at - tend thee, all through the night.

Guard - ian an - gels God will send thee, all through the night.

Soft the drows - y hours are creep - ing, hill and vale in slum - ber sleep - ing.

God, his lov - ing vig - il keep - ing, all through the night.

## Playing the Black Keys

Up to this point, you've been only playing the white keys. Let's add the black keys.

When moving from one key to the next, we've called that distance a *step*. An even smaller distance is played when moving from *one key to the very next key*, usually a white key to a black key. This smaller distance is called a *half step*.

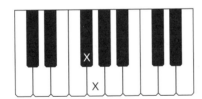  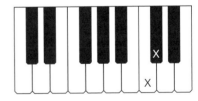

## Sharp

A half step *higher* (the very next key to the right on the keyboard) is called a sharp, and looks like this:

23

# Playing Sharps

"House of the Rising Sun" uses two sharps, G♯ and C♯. Note that the second C in measure eight will also be sharp, even though the sign only appears on the first of those two Cs. The note stays altered (sharp) for the entire measure.

Track 40

## House of the Rising Sun

Southern American Folksong

# A New Chord

Play the white keys A-C-E and you'll have an A minor chord. Much the same as Dm, Am has a darker sound quality than the major chords we've learned so far.

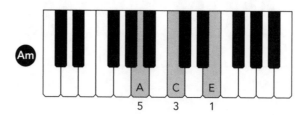

Track 41

Play the Am chord to hear this minor quality. Compare it to the Dm chord.

Our next song, "The Drunken Sailor" is an old, familiar, and spirited sea chantey. Look through the right-hand melody to find the F♯s in measures six and fourteen. Instead of white key F, play the black key to the very right, which is F♯. Use your third finger, the finger you would have used to play the white key. If reaching the black key is uncomfortable, slide your hand a little closer in, toward the back of the keyboard.

Let's look at a few other fingering cues. In measure five there are two half note Es. Play the first E with finger 5, and then switch fingers, playing the second E with finger 2. This allows you to continue up (ascend) the keyboard. As you come down (descend) the keyboard in measure seven, notice that finger 2 will cross over the thumb. This is new to you, but crossing over and under are very typical ways of moving up and down the keyboard.

# The Drunken Sailor

American Sea Chantey

Way, hey, up she ris - es! Pat - ent blocks o' dif - f'rent siz - es,

way, hey, up she ris - es ear - ly in the morn - in'!

What shall we do with a drunk - en sail - or? What shall we do with a drunk - en sail - or?

What shall we do with a drunk - en sail - or, ear - ly in the morn - in'?

Adding the left-hand chords will be easy! "The Drunken Sailor" uses only two chords, Am and G. In this song, play both chords in *root position*. That is, with the name of the chord as the bottom note. Since Am and G are right next to each other, you can easily shift from one chord to the next.

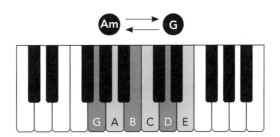

For keyboard diagrams of all the chords used in this book, refer to the Chord Index on page 75.

# Dotted Rhythms ▶

## Dotted Quarter Notes

A dot after a note adds half the value of the note itself. So far in this book you've played dotted half notes, which have the value of three beats:

$$\text{half note} \quad + \quad \text{dot} \quad = \quad \text{dotted half note}$$
$$2 \quad + \quad 1 \quad = \quad 3 \text{ beats}$$

Adding a dot to a quarter note adds half a beat, so the value of a dotted quarter note is one and one-half beats.

$$\text{quarter note} \quad + \quad \text{dot} \quad = \quad \text{dotted quarter note}$$
$$1 \quad + \quad \tfrac{1}{2} \quad = \quad 1\tfrac{1}{2} \text{ beats}$$

Dotted quarter notes are often followed by an eighth note, which by itself is one-half beat. A dotted quarter note plus an eighth note equals two full beats.

$$\text{dotted quarter} \quad + \quad \text{eighth} \quad = \quad 2 \text{ beats}$$

Sing or hum through the melody of "America," also known as "My Country 'Tis of Thee" to hear the dotted rhythm. Notice the counting provided under the notes in the first few measures. Following the lyrics will also help you feel the rhythm.

## Fingering Practice

Play through the right-hand part of this familiar patriotic tune to practice the fingering cues written in to help this song flow smoothly. Notice that your right hand will start with finger 2 on Middle C. This is so your thumb is ready to play the B below Middle C.

Most of the time your left hand will alternate between the C and G chords, but in the second to last measure you'll see an F chord. Changing chords on each of those beats will be a little tricky at first, but your ear will guide you. It won't take long for you to get used to the moves. Remember to slow down if you need more time to move from chord to chord.

# America

Words by Samuel Francis Smith
Music from *Thesaurus Musicus*

**Strongly**

## Flat

A half step *lower* (the very next key to the left on the keyboard) is called a *flat*, and looks like this:

## Natural

A *natural* cancels a previous sharp or flat.

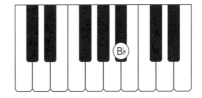

## A New Chord: B♭

The B♭ major chord is spelled B♭-D-F and played in this position:

The B♭ chord in "Deck the Halls" does not appear until the second-to-last measure. To move from the F chord to the B♭ chord, play F with finger 3, and play the D with finger 5, moving the thumb up to B♭.

# Caroling with a Flat

"Deck the Halls" includes flats, dotted quarter notes, and some tricky fingering moves. That's a lot of challenges for a simple carol! The familiar melody will help you along as you work on this tune.

First, let's take a look at the B♭ in measure one. Play that flat with finger 4, sliding your fingers a little closer to the back of the keyboard. As you complete the phrase, "la la la," notice that finger 2 crosses over the thumb. There's another crossing in measure 11, and again in the last measure. There's a natural sign in measure 11. This reminds us that the B in this measure is not flat, but natural. Play the right hand and sing along until you've got these fingerings figured out.

## Deck the Halls

Traditional Welsh Carol

# More Dotted Rhythms

"Auld Lang Syne" is a poem by the Scottish poet Robert Burns, set to a folk song from the British Isles. Historically sung on *Hogmanay* (New Years Eve in Scotland), the title translates to "days gone by."

The structure includes a repeated dotted rhythm, dotted quarter on beat one, followed by the eighth note. This feeling of long-short fits the poetry of the lyrics beautifully.

In measures seven and fifteen there are three left-hand chords. If switching between the chords that quickly proves difficult, you may omit the B♭ chord in brackets.

# Auld Lang Syne

Words by Robert Burns
Traditional Scottish Melody

Track 45

# More Syncopation

Track 46

Dotted quarter notes are often followed by an eighth note. In "Shenandoah" the eighth note comes first, followed by the dotted quarter note. This rhythm is another common syncopation. As you sing and play this melody, you'll feel yourself giving that first eighth note a little extra accent, feeling this very natural syncopation in a gentle way.

"Shenandoah" is a slow and wistful American folk song. Practice moving from the F chord to the Bb chord with your left hand, noticing the C chord in the next-to-last measure. Take the time you need at first to find these chords before adding the right hand.

# Shenandoah

Track 47

American Folk Song

"He's Got the Whole World in His Hands" has only two left-hand chords to play. This makes it easy to concentrate on the syncopated rhythms in the right-hand melody. We see more eighth-dotted quarter rhythms, as well as eighth-quarter-eighth.

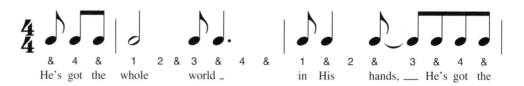

Let your ear help you out and sing along with this traditional spiritual. I've included three of the many verses, but if you know more, feel free to add as many as you like!

# He's Got the Whole World in His Hands

Track 48

Traditional Spiritual

## D.S. al Coda

In music, symbols can be used to show the *form* of the song, or organization of the notes. Some symbols indicate places that repeat and skip ahead. So far, you've used repeat signs, and 1st and 2nd ending signs. *D.S. al Coda* is another sign used to organize a piece of music.

D.S. al Coda means to return to the 𝄋, play until the words **To Coda** ⊕ and then skip to the place near the end of the music marked "coda." A coda is a separate ending section. (The Italian word coda means "tail," literally a "tail ending.")

Sing along as you play the right-hand melody. Identify the two flatted notes. Remember the rule that once a note is flat, it stays flat for the entire measure.

Track 50

# Rockin' Robin

Words and Music by J. Thomas

## Lesson 9 | 7th Chords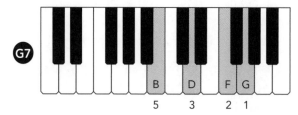

A *G7 chord* is simply a G chord with an added note. This added note is 7 notes higher than the root of the chord. Another way to think about it is that the added 7th is the note a whole step lower than the name of the chord.

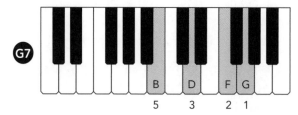

This ballpark favorite is harmonized with a G7 chord, and two new chords, A major and D major. Since you already know Dm and Am, these major chords will be easy. Only one note changes in each.

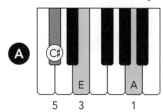 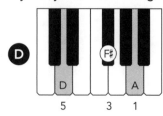

Track 51

# Take Me Out to the Ballgame

Words by Jack Norworth
Music by Albert von Tilzer

**Brightly**

Take me out to the ball - game,

take me out with the crowd. _____ Buy me some

pea - nuts and Crack - er Jack, I don't

care if I nev - er get back. Let me root, root,

root for the home team, if they don't win it's a

shame, _____ for it's one, two, three strikes, you're

out at the old ball - game. _____

32

# A New Symbol

A *fermata* is a musical sign that designates a note or chord be held longer than its written value. It often (although not always) is found near the end of a song, or phrase within a song, and creates a dramatic musical effect.

The performer decides exactly how long to hold the notes under a fermata. Experiment with this when you play the fermata in the last phrase of "For He's a Jolly Good Fellow."

## For He's a Jolly Good Fellow

Traditional

Track 52

# D.C. al Coda

Track 53

We've already learned the music symbol D.S. al coda. D.C. al coda is very similar. D.C. stands for *da capo*, or "the head." When you see a D.C. al coda sign, return to the *beginning* of the song (the head), play until the "To Coda" sign and then jump ahead to the coda to finish the song.

"Guantanamera" is a familiar Cuban folksong harmonized with just three chords: C, F and G7.

Track 54

## Guantanamera

Cuban Folksong

# G7 in a Minor Key

So far you've moved to the G7 chord from C major, a chord pattern that's become very familiar to you. In "Wayfaring Stranger" the G7 chord follows an F chord. The note both chords have in common is F. Keep finger 2 on F and move your thumb down to the G. Finger 5 moves down to B and finger 3 plays D. Practice shifting between the F and G7 chords until you can play both chords easily.

# Chord Inversions

Earlier you've played the Am minor chord in root position, with the A on the bottom. For our next song, "Wayfaring Stranger," we'll use a different *inversion*, or arrangement of the notes. Chords are played in various inversions to make it easier to move from chord to chord.

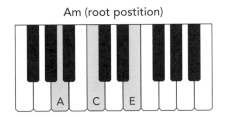

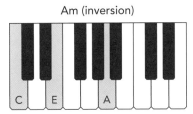

Playing the A minor chord with C on the bottom makes it easier to play when moving to and from the other chords in this song.

# Wayfaring Stranger

Track 55

Southern American Folk Hymn

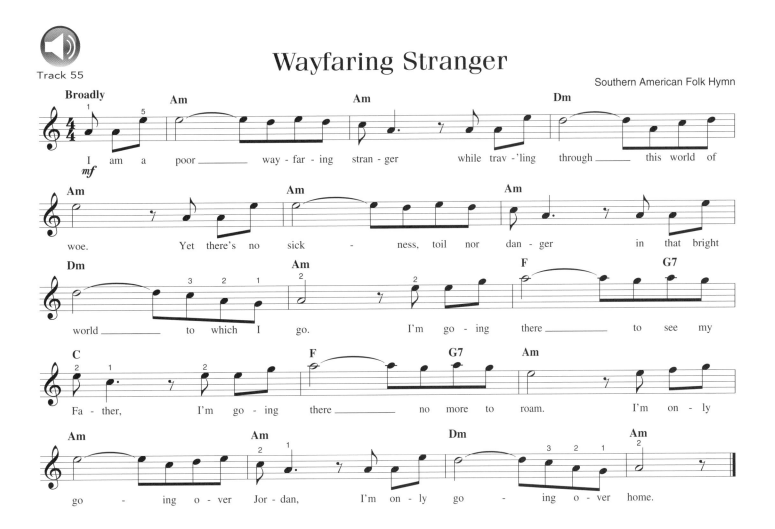

# Scales and Keys

## Major Scale

Track 56

A musical *scale* is an arrangement of notes in a specific pattern of half and whole steps. Just like the various types of chords, there are several different kinds of scales. The most familiar and maybe most identifiable is the *major* scale. Take a moment to play the eight white keys, C-D-E-F-G-A-B-C, from low to high. You've just played a C major scale!

Let's take a closer look at the pattern of notes that make up a major scale. What gives the scale its distinctive sound is the pattern of whole steps and half steps. This pattern is:

Whole step – Whole step – Half step – Whole step – Whole step – Whole step – Half step

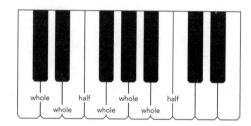

As you can see by the example, a half step on the keyboard is the distance between one key to the very next key. Most of the time this distance is a white key to a black key. However, the white key pairs E-F, and B-C are also half steps. Whole steps are larger. On the piano they can be described as one key to the next with a key in between.

Most melodies use notes from a particular scale, with the *tonic* note of the scale often found at the end. This tonic note gives the scale its name, and acts as the home base for the rest of the notes. The name of the scale is also the name of the *key* a song is written in. So a song written using the notes of the C major scale is in the *key of C major*.

## Caroling with a Scale

The classic Christmas tune "Joy to the "World" begins with a *descending* (high to low) C major scale. As you play, notice the other scale-like phrases that use smaller sections of the scale.

# Joy to the World

Words by Isaac Watts
Music by George Frideric Handel
Adapted by Lowell Mason

Track 57

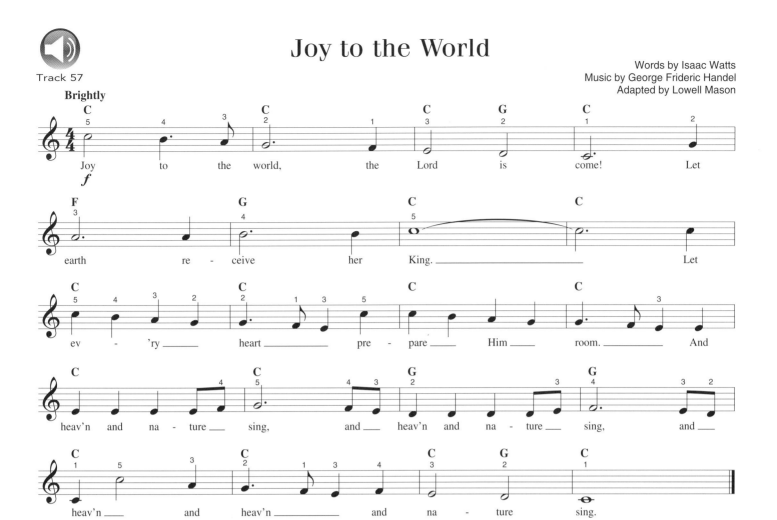

## Minor Scale

Track 58

Playing all white keys from C to C creates a major scale. Playing all white keys from A to A creates a *minor* scale, which has a different pattern of whole and half steps, and a different sound.

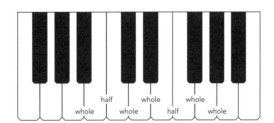

There is an interesting combination of major and minor chords in "Scarborough Fair." Play through the chords with your left hand to hear the difference between the major and minor tonalities.

# Scarborough Fair

Traditional English

## Blues Scale

The *blues* scale is related to the minor scale, with a slightly different pattern of whole and half steps.

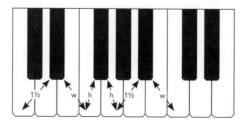

Notice the places where the notes are one and one-half steps apart. Look out for flats, sharps, and naturals as you play this scale with your right hand.

## Swing Eighths

Blues or Jazz styles often use a rhythm called swing eighths. This is a type of skipping rhythm in which groups of two eighth notes are played with a "long-short" feel, rather than two equal eighths. This style is often designated with the tempo "Shuffle" or the symbol:

$$( \; \flat\flat \; = \; \overset{3}{\flat\flat}\flat \; )$$

Play the blues scale again, this time with swing eighths. Listen to the audio example to get a feel for the "swing" sound.

## Playing the Blues

A style of music known as the *12-Bar Blues* uses the blues scale over a specific chord pattern. "Swingin' Blues" uses this pattern. The harmony in a basic 12-bar blues pattern is very simple, allowing room for improvisation in the melody. Be sure to swing the eighth notes in the right hand, and, as you become comfortable with the blues scale, try improvising as you play along with the audio.

Track 61

## Swingin' Blues

By Bad Bones Davis

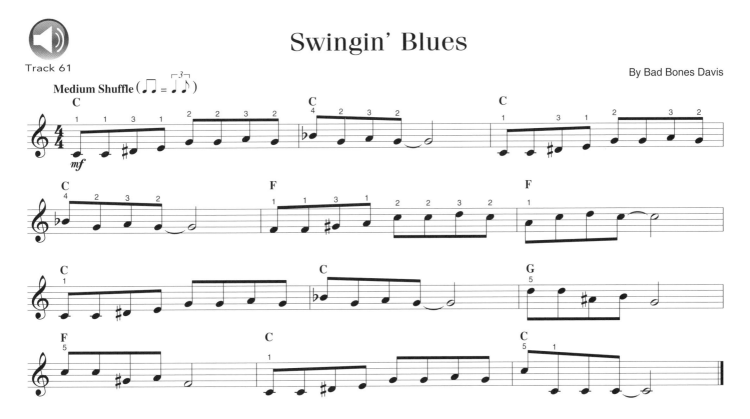

# More Chords

## Augmented Chords

An *augmented* chord is a major chord with the fifth note of the scale raised a half step. It is notated with a + to designate this raised note.

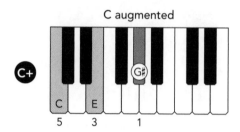

Play a C major chord with your left hand. Slide your thumb up one half step to the G♯ to play a C augmented chord. Practice moving from C to C+ as you listen to the difference in sound between the two chords. The spiritual "Deep River" is harmonized with a C+ chord that appears in the first measure, and then again in four additional measures throughout the song.

## Em Chord

There's another new chord to learn in this southern classic, the Em chord. This chord uses three white keys, and is played in this inversion.

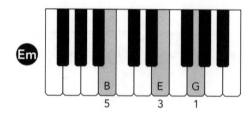

If you are familiar with "Deep River," try singing along as your left hand practices the chord changes. If you don't know this tune, leave out the left hand and learn the melody first. Don't let the high ledger line C catch you by surprise. It's just an octave (eight notes) higher than the previous C.

# Deep River

African-American Spiritual
Based on Joshua 3

Track 62

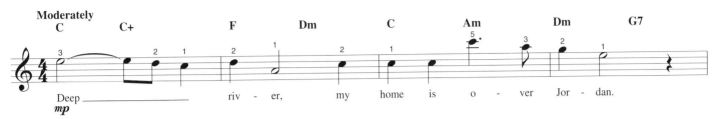

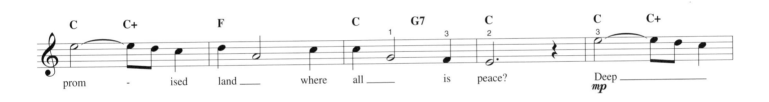

# New 7th Chord

Remember that 7th chords are created by adding the 7th note of the scale. You've been playing G7 for a while now, so let's add a new 7th chord: D7. The D major chord is spelled D-F♯-A. To make it a 7th chord, add C. Let's play this chord with the C as the lowest note.

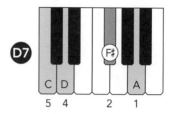

This makes it easy to play following a C chord, as you will find it in our next tune, "Chicago (That Toddlin' Town)." Practice moving from C to D7 in this inversion.

# One More Chord

There's one more new chord to learn in "Chicago (That Toddlin' Town)" but it's an easy one. Play E major in this inversion.

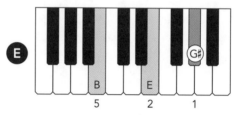

# A Syncopated Classic

Track 63

If you're not familiar with this oldie, listen to the audio track before you play it, or check out Frank Sinatra's iconic recording. Sometimes syncopated music looks more difficult that it sounds. Ties and dotted rhythms give this tune its jazzy feel.

Notice the *cue notes* in measure four, and again in measure twenty. These smaller size notes often show an echo (as they do here) or alternate melody. You might think about playing them a bit softer than the melody, to produce that echo effect.

With the variety of chords harmonizing this tune, you'll want to spend some time practicing your left hand alone. Moving from C to D7 in line three will be fairly easy to do if you're looking ahead to prepare for it. In line six, pay special attention to moving from G7 to E, and then from E to Am. Move from Am to A major in the next measure by changing C to C♯, mimicking the movement in the right-hand melody. Play this up-tempo number with a bit of swing!

# Chicago (That Toddlin' Town)

Words and Music by Fred Fisher

# Diminished and Diminished 7th Chords

A *diminished* chord is a minor chord with the fifth note of the scale lowered a half step. A diminished chord is notated with the word "dim" after the note name. Play a B diminished chord, as illustrated below.

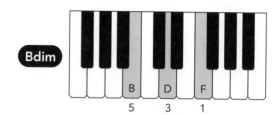

A *diminished 7th* chord is created by adding a 7th to an already diminished chord. This chord is written with "dim7" after the note name. Try adding the 7th to the Bdim chord below.

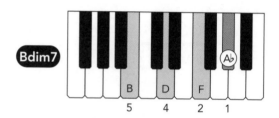

# A Little Bit of Everything

"Bill Bailey, Won't You Please Come Home" is a Dixieland favorite from the early 1900s, and is still popular today. Harmonically there's a little bit of everything in this lively tune; major, minor, augmented and diminished chords, as well as 7th chords. There's only one more new chord, Gm: G-B♭-D. We'll play it in the inversion below.

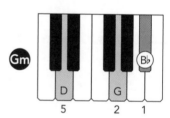

Spend some time with the left hand alone to work out the chords. You'll notice right away that you really don't have to move your left hand much in order to play everything. When you have two or more measures without a chord change, feel free to repeat the chord, especially if you hear the harmony starting to fade away.

# Bill Bailey,
# Won't You Please Come Home

Words and Music by Hughie Cannon

# Music Review

So far we've learned the basics of reading music on the treble clef. Let's review treble clef before we shift our focus to the bass clef.

## Note Values

Music is written with symbols called **notes**. Each type of note has a specific rhythmic value. When the quarter note gets one beat, all other rhythmic values are determined by the quarter note.

quarter note = 1 beat

half note = 2 beats

dotted half note = 3 beats

whole note = 4 beats

## Staff

Notes are placed on a **staff**, five horizontal lines and four spaces. Placement of these notes on the staff determines pitch, how high or low the note will sound. The higher the note is placed on the staff, the higher it will sound; the lower the note is placed on the staff, the lower it will sound. Since not all notes will fit on just five lines and four spaces, **ledger lines** are used to extend the staff.

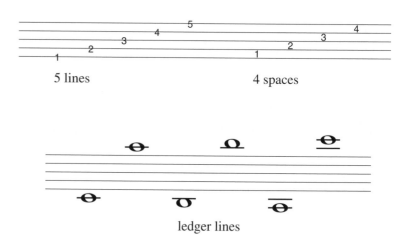

5 lines          4 spaces

ledger lines

## Clef

A symbol called a **clef** indicates where the notes will be played on the keyboard. The right hand plays notes written in the **treble** clef. Let's review the names of the treble clef notes.

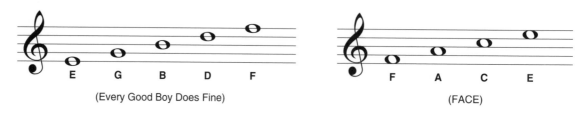

E    G    B    D    F

(Every Good Boy Does Fine)

F    A    C    E

(FACE)

# Rhythm

To organize the notes on the staff into **measures**, **bar lines** are used. A **time signature** determines how many beats will be in each measure. The top number of the time signature indicates the number of beats per measure, and the bottom number names the note that gets one beat.

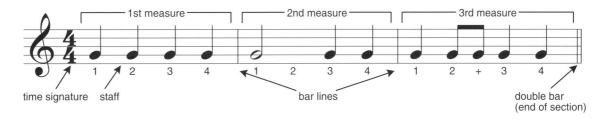

# Intervals

Notes move along the staff in patterns of steps, skips, and larger intervals. Repeated notes stay on the same line or space; larger intervals skip one or more lines and spaces. Study the intervals written on the staff below.

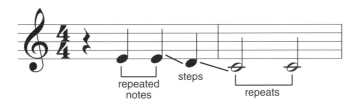

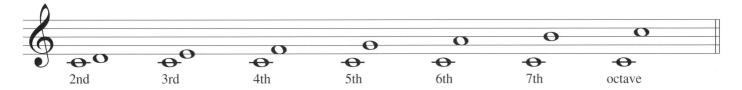

# Treble Clef Sight Reading Review

Play this tune in treble clef with your right hand, looking for steps, skips, and larger intervals.

## Simple Waltz

Track 66

**Moderately**

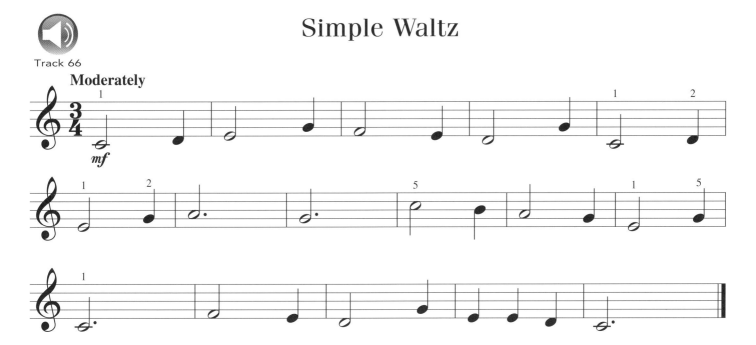

# Bass Clef

The focus so far has been on reading the treble clef and playing melody with the right hand. To be a well-rounded keyboard player it's important to be able to read the bass clef, and to have equal strength and dexterity in both hands.

## The Bass Clef

As you know, the clef sign determines the pitches written on the staff. The **bass staff** looks like this:

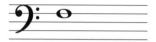

The fourth line, which falls between the two dots of the clef sign, is designated as the pitch F; the first F below middle C. Because it designates the pitch F, this clef can also be called the **F clef**. Take a few moments to study the pitches written on the bass staff. Note that the names of the lines and spaces written in bass clef are NOT the same as the treble clef!

G B D F A

(Good Birds Don't Fly Alone)

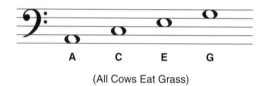

A C E G

(All Cows Eat Grass)

## Bass Clef Note-Reading Practice

Scan the line of bass clef notes below. Set a timer. How quickly can you name the notes? Set the timer again. How quickly can you name, and then play the notes?

## C Position for Left Hand

Five consecutive notes in a row, played by five consecutive fingers, is sometimes referred to as a "five-finger position," acting as a home base of sorts for simple tunes. Study the notes in C position below, written on the bass staff.

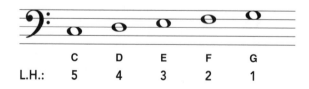

| L.H.: | C | D | E | F | G |
|---|---|---|---|---|---|
| | 5 | 4 | 3 | 2 | 1 |

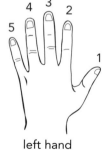

left hand

The popular Christmas tune "Jingle Bells" uses the five notes in C position. Once you've learned this securely with left hand, try adding right hand an octave higher. Playing the same part with both hands is called playing in **unison**.

# Jingle Bells

Track 67

Words and Music by J. Pierpont

You're ready to play Beethoven's famous theme "Ode to Joy" from Symphony No. 9. Place left hand finger 5 on the C below middle C, with consecutive fingers on the notes that follow. Notice whether the notes repeat, move up by step, or down by step.

# Ode to Joy
## (Theme from Symphony No. 9)

Track 68

By Ludwig van Beethoven

**Moderately**

# Left Hand as Equal Partner

Even though right hand plays the melody much of the time in music written for piano, the left hand plays a far more important role than mere support. Accompaniments such as chords, arpeggios, and rhythmic patterns require a strong technique and comfort in moving around the keyboard.

## Left Hand Warm-ups

Use the C position to play the following exercise. Play slowly at first, and as you feel comfortable, increase the tempo.

Track 69

**Moderately**

Play this exercise in the G position, and then the F position.

Track 70

**Moderately**

Track 71

**Moderately**

## Left Hand Chords on the Bass Staff

So far, chords have been notated using chord labels above the treble staff. Chords can also be notated on the bass staff. Here's an example of chords written on the bass staff. As you play the chords, listen for all the notes of the chord to sound at the same time. Pick your hand up as needed to move to each chord.

Track 72

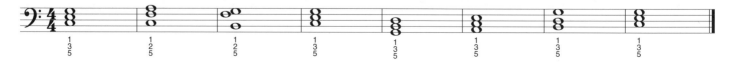

Track 73

The chords you just played could be called **blocked chords**, as all the notes are played together, in a block. When written this way they even look a bit like a block, with all the notes stacked up on the staff. **Broken chords** are the opposite. Instead of playing the notes all together, they're played one note at a time. Broken chords are also called **arpeggios**.

# Rhythmic Riffs and Accompaniments

Sometimes the left hand really gets to shine! Whether taking a turn at the melody, or playing a fun groove, the left hand can add a lot of style.

## Jazzy Walking Bass

Track 74

## Cool R&B

Track 75

## Classic Rock Bass

Track 76

Challenge: improvise a right-hand melody or chords over the left-hand examples you just played.

# The Grand Staff

Most piano music is written on the **grand staff**. The grand staff is made up of the treble staff and the bass staff connected with a bracket. When reading the grand staff, the right hand plays the treble staff and the left hand plays the bass staff.

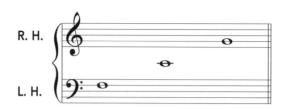

## Playing on the Grand Staff

Play "Ode to Joy" notated on the Grand Staff. Notice that the melody moves from treble staff (right hand) to bass staff (left hand).

# Ode to Joy

Track 77

By Ludwig van Beethoven

Set a steady quarter note beat before you play "Alouette," so the eighth notes are right in time.
Remember, two eighth notes are equal to one quarter note.

# Alouette

Traditional

Track 78

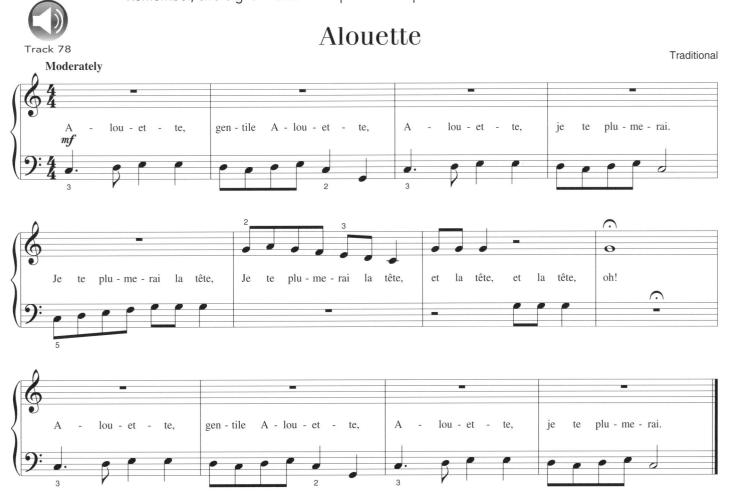

## Tempo and Dynamics Review

Find the tempo indication at the beginning of the song, right above the time signature. Look for
dynamics and other expression marks in the music throughout. See the box below for a quick review.

| Dynamics and Expression | | |
|---|---|---|
| *p* | piano | soft |
| *f* | forte | loud |
| *mp* | mezzo piano | moderately soft |
| *mf* | mezzo forte | moderately loud |
| *rit.* | ritardando | slowing down |
| *a tempo* | | return to original tempo |
| | Crescendo (cresc.) | gradually get louder |
| | Decresendo (decresc.) | gradually get softer |
| | Slur | play smoothly; connected |
| | Staccato | play detached |

# Playing Hands Together

"Yankee Doodle" begins with left hand playing melody. In measure 9, melody switches to right hand, and the left hand harmonizes with C and G, ending with both hands playing melody together in the last two measures.

## Yankee Doodle

Track 79

Traditional

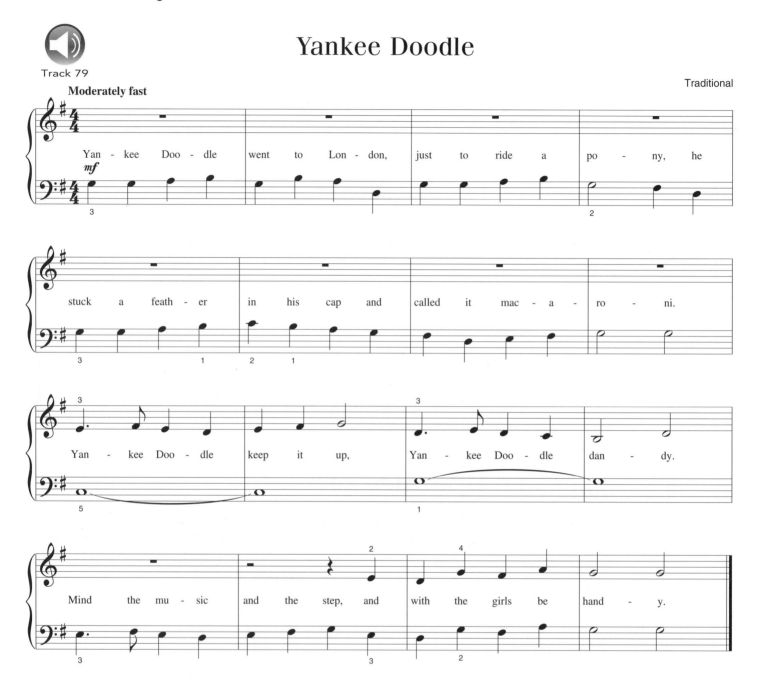

# Key Signature Review

Sharps or flats placed immediately to the right of the clef sign are called the **key signature**, and determine the key, or tonal center of the song. Those sharps or flats named in the key signature are altered for the entire song.

# Strategies for Playing Hands Together

When learning to play songs notated on the grand staff, it sometimes helps to study each staff separately. If you're unsure about bass staff notes, this is the time to really review and learn the left-hand part. Sometimes it's the right-hand part that could be challenging, especially if there are many hand-position shifts or fingering changes. When in doubt, it's always a good idea to practice each hand alone. Let's look at some specific examples.

## Strategies

"Bravery" is a classical piece by 18th century composer Daniel Gottlob Türk. There are fewer notes to play in the left hand, so let's start with the bass staff.

Beginning with left-hand thumb on middle C, you will not have to move your hand until the very last measure, when you stretch your 5th finger down to reach the low C. Play the bass staff part with your left hand now, being sure to hold each whole note for four counts.

Before you play the right-hand part, glance through the measures looking for any moves or shifts. In this case, right hand stays in one place for the entire piece. Play the right-hand part alone until you've learned the melody securely.

Play both hands together. Before you begin, choose a tempo that will allow you to play easily and without pausing or stopping. Are there places you need to go back to review? Try hands together again or isolate a spot that might be difficult or confusing. "Bravery" is marked "Moderato." Can you play this piece easily at a moderate tempo?

## Bravery

Track 80

By Daniel Gottlob Türk

"America," sometimes known as "My Country, 'Tis of Thee," has a well-known melody played by the right hand. Review the melody, noting the hand shifts and fingering changes. Play the left-hand part alone. How many different notes are in the bass staff? Play hands together slowly at first. You may wish to sing as you play to help propel you along.

# America

Words by Samuel Francis Smith
Music from *Thesaurus Musicus*

Track 81

## More Strategies

Don't be intimidated by left-hand parts that contain more than one note at a time. Usually these are easier to read than you think. Analyze the intervals and look for notes that stay the same from one interval (or measure) to the next. Let's take a look at the bass staff of "Largo from Symphony No. 9 ("New World")." Play these first eight measures, taking note of the intervals marked.

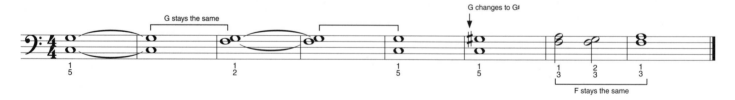

The next eight measures contain only two different thirds that alternate.

# Largo from Symphony No. 9
## ("New World")

By Antonin Dvořák

# Left-Hand Accompaniment Patterns

You may be starting to notice that often the left hand is quite patterned. Learning to recognize common accompaniment patterns can make reading the bass staff easier.

## Chords

You've had some experience with chordal accompaniment already, in "Largo from Symphony No. 9 ("New World")." Chordal accompaniments can be quite static or move around greatly. The chords themselves can change at a slow rate or quickly. In the example below, left hand plays just four chords, moving down a key each time. Each chord gets two beats in the first two measures, and then the chords double in speed when they change to quarter notes.

Track 83

## Arpeggios

Arpeggios (broken chords) are also a frequent accompaniment pattern. Remember, "broken" chords are full chords played one note at a time instead of all together.

Track 84

## Independent Lines

Sometimes the left-hand part is entirely independent of the right-hand part. It may be melodic, or fully harmonic, and more complex than a blocked or broken chord.

Sight-read the bass staff measures below. Note the fingering. When learning a piece with entirely independent lines, both lines must be secure before playing them together.

Track 85

# Putting It Together

## Chordal Accompaniment

Playing blocked chords is an easy way to give a full sound to a simple melody on the piano. Add the chord pattern you just practiced in Lesson 17 to "The Cat Came Back."

Track 86

## The Cat Came Back

Words and Music by Harry S. Miller

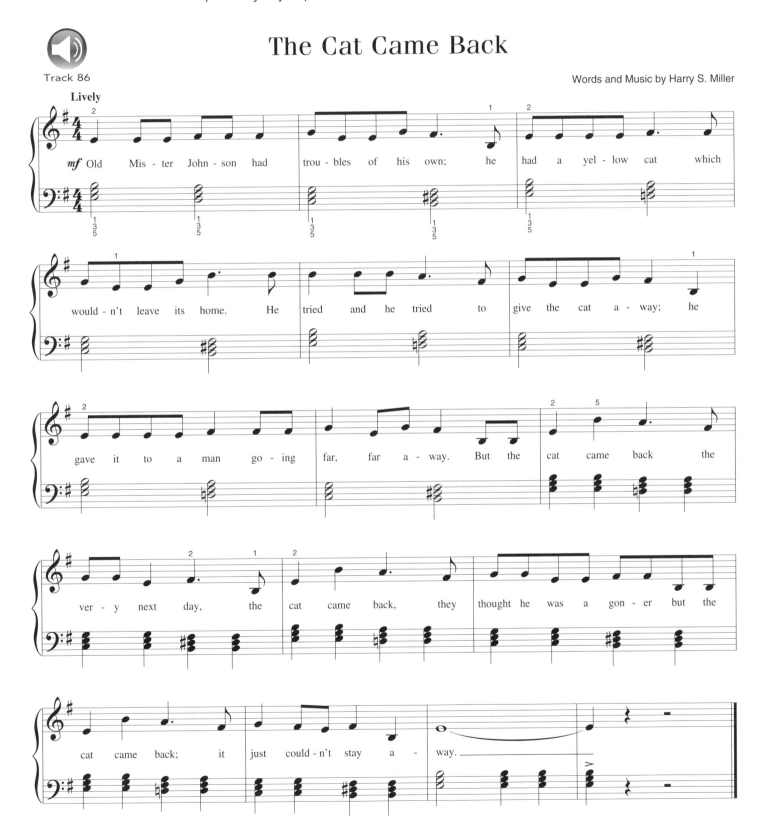

# Arpeggiated Accompaniment

"Du, Du Liegst Mir Im Herzen (You, You Weigh on My Heart)" is a lovely German folk song with an arpeggiated (broken chord) accompaniment. Notice that for most of the song, you are only playing two chords in the left hand, C and G7. The G7 chord has B as the root (or lowest) note of the chord. Look ahead to the last eight measures. Here the broken chords change to blocked chords for contrast.

## Du, Du Liegst Mir Im Herzen
### (You, You Weigh on My Heart)

German Folksong

Track 87

# Independent Lines

"Little Invention" is short but complex. Both hands play melodic lines that intertwine. Learn each hand carefully before playing hands together. Challenge yourself! Sing one line while playing the other line.

## Little Invention

Track 88

By Jakub Jan Ryba

The left hand echoes the right hand for the first four measures of "A Conversation." Here again, you'll want to learn each hand alone before playing hands together. After taking the repeat under the first ending bracket, skip those first ending measures to take the second ending.

## A Conversation

Track 89

By Béla Bartók

# Lesson 19 Bass Lines and the Blues

Groovy bass lines are one of the most fun things to play with left hand. Whether it's a repeated chord pattern, "walking" bass, or just a jazzy little riff, these are places the left hand can really shine.

The left-hand part in "Hesitation Blues" is quite simple. There are two places where the left hand adds some interest. In measures 5-6 the eighth-dotted-quarter rhythm echoes the right hand and pushes the beat along.

Under the first and second ending brackets the left hand has a little riff to play. Practice moving from the B♭ to B♮.

Track 90

## Hesitation Blues

Words and Music by Billy Smythe
and J. Scott Middleton

The left-hand part in "Freight Train" is so much fun to play! Take a look at the opening measures.

The D chord is outlined, with a bit of a "walk" up the scale in measure 2. The A chord is outlined starting in measure 5, and the F#7 chord in measures 11-12. Practice playing each of these patterns with your left hand on its own before you play the whole song.

# Freight Train

Words and Music by
Elizabeth Cotten

Track 91

The driving left-hand 5ths and 6ths give "Worried Man Blues" its old-timey character. Use fingers 2 and 5 to play the fifth so you can switch to fingers 1 and 5 on the sixth. Don't be afraid to lean into the eighth note whenever the eighth-dotted-quarter note rhythm occurs. Take your time with this lazy blues and let the lyrics tell the story.

# Worried Man Blues

Traditional

Track 92

# Coordination and Syncopation

The ability to move smoothly from one hand to the other or play different notes and rhythms in each hand at the same time is crucial as you advance to more difficult music. Here are a few simple exercises to strengthen both your fingers and coordination skills.

## Five-Note Scale Exercises

As the five-note scale moves from left hand to right hand, make sure the tempo flows smoothly without a pause. Choose a slow tempo first, and gradually increase to a faster tempo.

Track 93

This next exercise is a bit trickier. If you play each hand separately, you'll see that both play a simple 5-note scale. Play as slowly as necessary to keep the tempo steady, without stopping or pausing.

Track 94

Both of these exercises can be played with variations:

- Right hand staccato, left hand legato
- Left hand staccato, right hand legato
- Right hand forte, left hand piano
- Left hand forte, right hand piano

"Für Elise" is one of Beethoven's most famous keyboard pieces. One of the challenges when performing this piece is to smoothly connect the notes in a singing manner, and also to smoothly connect the notes as they move between the hands. The arrangement below is abridged and simplified, but still allows you to practice these important techniques while enjoying this classic melody.

# Für Elise

By Ludwig van Beethoven

## Practice tips for Für Elise

1. Notice the left-hand patterns. In measures 2-9 there are two alternating measures in the left hand. Measures 10-11 are different. Practice the left-hand part alone.

2. Work with the hairpin *crescendo* and *decrescendo* to help shape the right-hand phrase. Listen for a smooth, connected sound that rises and falls.

3. Playing hands together, think ahead as each hand "trades off" within the measure.

4. In measures 13-15, keep counting eighth notes as you alternate E in each hand.

5. Play this piece at a slow tempo until all notes and rhythms are secure and easy to play.

## Syncopation

**Syncopation** occurs when weak beats are accented. A very common syncopation is the eighth-quarter-eighth rhythm found in the arrangement of "He's Got the Whole World in His Hands" on the next page. Right hand plays the syncopated melody against a steady rhythm in left hand. Knowing each part securely is necessary to perform this song confidently.

Singing along will help you get comfortable with the melody. Challenge yourself to count aloud, subdividing the right-hand part in eighth notes: "one-and-two-and-three-and-four-and" for even more security.

In the second half of the arrangement, left hand switches to a fun walking bass line. Practice this alone at first, looking out for accidentals and fingering shifts. If playing hands together here is challenging, try tapping the rhythm hands together as you count aloud, lining up the eighth notes against the steady quarter notes. Slow down the tempo as needed.

# He's Got the Whole World in His Hands

Traditional Spiritual

# Highlighting the Left Hand

In this simplified version of "Moonlight" Sonata Theme, both hands play a continuous broken-chord pattern. Right hand introduces the pattern, and then switches to melody in measure 10. At measure 11 left hand plays broken chords supporting the right-hand melody. The chords change frequently but moves are minimal.

## "Moonlight" Sonata Theme

Track 97

By Ludwig van Beethoven

Notice the ( ♫ = ♪♪ ) after the tempo head designating swing eighths in "Midnight Special." This creates an eighth-note feel of "long-short" adding to the bluesy character of this classic. Identify the chord changes and practice moving from chord to chord as the harmony shifts in the left hand before adding the right hand. Once you know where you're going, relax and let the left hand drive this tune.

# Midnight Special

Track 98

Railroad Song

The traditional Scottish "Skye Boat Song" beginning on p. 72 exemplifies how much impact strong left-hand writing can have. While the left hand never plays the melody, it supports the right hand with flowing accompaniment, provides rhythmic interest with a syncopated section, and finally, leaves the listener with a feeling a peace and strength through the use of blocked intervals. Divide this arrangement into sections as you learn each accompaniment style, first with left hand, adding right hand when left hand is secure.

# Skye Boat Song

Traditional Scottish

**Flowing along**

*mp*

*poco rit.*

With pedal

*mf* *a tempo*

*mf*

*f*

Left hand plays melody in "Night Escape." Use the long slurs to help identify and shape each phrase. Practicing one phrase at a time is an excellent way to learn this piece carefully. First play the melody, using the fingering given and listening for a smooth, legato sound. Study the right-hand chords. There are seven different chords to play; always seconds or thirds with minimal movement. Work through the slight shifts and changes in each phrase of the right-hand part, playing hands together only after each hand is well understood and comfortable. Practice at a super slow tempo at first. When you can play confidently at a slow tempo it will be easy to increase the tempo. As you work on each phrase, also note the dynamics.

# Night Escape

By Cornelius Gurlitt

# Chord Index

## Major Chords

 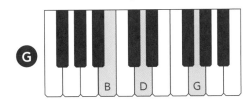 or

  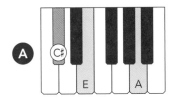

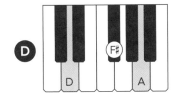 

## Minor Chords

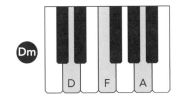  or

 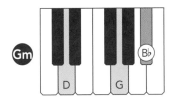

## Seventh Chords

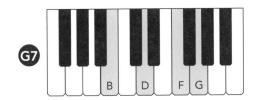 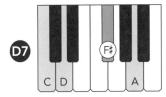

## Augmented Chord

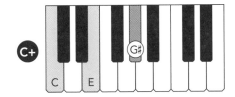

## Diminshed 7th Chord

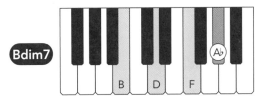

# Glossary of Musical Terms

| | |
|---|---|
| **Augmented Chord** | A major chord with a raised fifth. |
| **Bar Lines** | Lines used to divide the staff into measures. |
| **Chord** | Three or more notes played together at the same time. |
| **Coda** | Section at the end of a piece of music, which brings the piece to a close. |
| **Cue Notes** | Small sized notes that indicate an alternate part. |
| **D.C. al Coda** | An indication to return to the beginning of the song; play until **To Coda** ⊕ skipping to the coda to finish the song. D.C. stands for the Italian words, "da capo" which mean "the head." |
| **D.S. al Coda** | An indication to return to the sign 𝄋 and play until **To Coda** ⊕ skipping to the coda to finish the song. D.S. stands for the Italian words "del segno" which mean "the sign." |
| **Diminished Chord** | A minor chord with a lowered fifth. |
| **Dotted Half Note** | 𝅗𝅥. A note three beats long in 4/4 time. The dot adds half the value of the note it follows. |
| **Double Bar Line** | Indicates the end of a piece. |
| **Dynamics** | Symbols indicating degrees of loud and soft. |
| **Eighth Note** | ♪ Half the value of a quarter note, two or more can be joined by a beam: ♫ Two eighth notes equal one quarter note. |
| **Fermata** | ⌢ Symbol used to hold a note or rest for longer than its notated value. |
| **Flat** | ♭ Lowers a note a half step for an entire measure. |
| **Half Note** | 𝅗𝅥 Receives two beats in 4/4 time, equal in length to two quarter notes. |
| **Inversion** | An arrangement of notes in a chord when the root of the chord is not the lowest note. |
| **Lead Sheet** | Style of notation in which the melody is written in the treble clef, with chord symbols above the staff. |
| **Ledger Lines** | Short lines used to extend the staff higher or lower. |
| **Major Chord** | A chord with a root, major third and perfect fifth. |
| **Measure** | Space between two bar lines containing the number of beats determined by the time signature. |
| **Middle C** | The C nearest the middle of the keyboard. |
| **Minor Chord** | A chord with a root, lowered third, and fifth. |

| | | |
|---|---|---|
| **Natural** | ♮ | Cancels a previous sharp or flat. |
| **Notes** | | Symbols that represent sound. |
| **Octave** | | Distance from one note to eight notes higher or lower. |
| **Pick-up Notes** | | One or more notes before the first full measure, also called "upbeats." |
| **Pitch** | | The highness or lowness of a sound. |
| **Quarter Note** | ♩ | Receives one beat. There are 4 quarter notes in a 4/4 measure. |
| **Repeat Sign** | 𝄆 | Repeat a section, or entire piece of music from the beginning. |
| **Rests** | | Symbols that represent silence. |
| **Rhythm** | | Duration of notes and rests. |
| **Root Position** | | Chord in which the name of the chord (the root) is the lowest note. |
| **Scale** | | A sequence of notes in ascending or descending order. |
| **Seventh Chord** | | Chord built with the root, third, fifth and seventh. |
| **Sharp** | ♯ | Raises a note a half step for an entire measure. |
| **Skip** | | On the keyboard, the distance from one key to another, skipping a key in between; on the staff, a note that moves from line to line, or space to space. |
| **Staff** | | Five horizontal lines and four spaces; note placement on the staff determines how high or low the note will sound. |
| **Step** | | On the keyboard, the distance from one key to the next; on the staff, a note written on a line to a note written on the next space. |
| **Swing Eighths** | | Rhythm in which groups of eighth notes are given a "long-short" feel, often indicated by: ♫ = ♩♪ |
| **Syncopation** | | The placement of accents on beats not usually accented. |
| **Tie** | | A curved line connecting two notes of the same pitch. A tie between the notes gives the first note the value of both notes "tied" together. |
| **Time Signature** | | Symbol indicating how many beats per measure; determines what type of note receives one beat. |
| **Treble Clef** | | Designates the second line of the staff as the note G, also called the G clef. |
| **Whole note** | 𝅝 | Lasts four beats, or a complete measure in 4/4 time. |

# Play Today! Series

## The Ultimate Self-Teaching Series

These are complete guides to the basics, designed to offer quality instruction, terrific songs, and professional-quality audio with tons of full-demo tracks and instruction. Each book includes over 70 great songs and examples!

## Play Accordion Today!
| | | |
|---|---|---|
| 00701744 | Level 1 Book/Audio | $10.99 |
| 00702657 | Level 1 Songbook Book/Audio | $12.99 |

## Play Alto Sax Today!
| | | |
|---|---|---|
| 00842049 | Level 1 Book/Audio | $9.99 |
| 00842050 | Level 2 Book/Audio | $9.99 |
| 00320359 | DVD | $14.95 |
| 00842051 | Songbook Book/Audio | $12.95 |
| 00699555 | Beginner's – Level 1 Book/Audio & DVD | $19.95 |
| 00699492 | Play Today Plus Book/Audio | $14.95 |

## Play Banjo Today!
| | | |
|---|---|---|
| 00699897 | Level 1 Book/Audio | $9.99 |
| 00701006 | Level 2 Book/Audio | $9.99 |
| 00320913 | DVD | $14.99 |
| 00115999 | Songbook Book/Audio | $12.99 |
| 00701873 | Beginner's – Level 1 Book/Audio & DVD | $19.95 |

## Play Bass Today!
| | | |
|---|---|---|
| 00842020 | Level 1 Book/Audio | $9.99 |
| 00842036 | Level 2 Book/Audio | $9.99 |
| 00320356 | DVD | $14.95 |
| 00842037 | Songbook Book/Audio | $12.95 |
| 00699552 | Beginner's – Level 1 Book/Audio & DVD | $19.99 |

## Play Cello Today!
| | | |
|---|---|---|
| 00151353 | Level 1 Book/Audio | $9.99 |

## Play Clarinet Today!
| | | |
|---|---|---|
| 00842046 | Level 1 Book/Audio | $9.99 |
| 00842047 | Level 2 Book/Audio | $9.99 |
| 00320358 | DVD | $14.95 |
| 00842048 | Songbook Book/Audio | $12.95 |
| 00699554 | Beginner's – Level 1 Book/Audio & DVD | $19.95 |
| 00699490 | Play Today Plus Book/Audio | $14.95 |

## Play Dobro Today!
| | | |
|---|---|---|
| 00701505 | Level 1 Book/Audio | $9.99 |

## Play Drums Today!
| | | |
|---|---|---|
| 00842021 | Level 1 Book/Audio | $9.99 |
| 00842038 | Level 2 Book/Audio | $9.95 |
| 00320355 | DVD | $14.95 |
| 00842039 | Songbook Book/Audio | $12.95 |
| 00699551 | Beginner's – Level 1 Book/Audio & DVD | $19.95 |
| 00703291 | Starter | $24.99 |

## Play Flute Today
| | | |
|---|---|---|
| 00842043 | Level 1 Book/Audio | $9.95 |
| 00842044 | Level 2 Book/Audio | $9.99 |
| 00320360 | DVD | $14.95 |
| 00842045 | Songbook Book/Audio | $12.95 |
| 00699553 | Beginner's – Level 1 Book/Audio & DVD | $19.95 |

## Play Guitar Today!
| | | |
|---|---|---|
| 00696100 | Level 1 Book/Audio | $9.99 |
| 00696101 | Level 2 Book/Audio | $9.99 |
| 00320353 | DVD | $14.95 |
| 00696102 | Songbook Book/Audio | $12.99 |
| 00699544 | Beginner's – Level 1 Book/Audio & DVD | $19.95 |
| 00702431 | Worship Songbook Book/Audio | $12.99 |
| 00695662 | Complete Kit | $29.95 |

## Play Harmonica Today!
| | | |
|---|---|---|
| 00700179 | Level 1 Book/Audio | $9.99 |
| 00320653 | DVD | $14.99 |
| 00701875 | Beginner's – Level 1 Book/Audio & DVD | $19.95 |

## Play Mandolin Today!
| | | |
|---|---|---|
| 00699911 | Level 1 Book/Audio | $9.99 |
| 00320909 | DVD | $14.99 |
| 00115029 | Songbook Book/Audio | $12.99 |
| 00701874 | Beginner's – Level 1 Book/Audio & DVD | $19.99 |

## Play Piano Today!
## Revised Edition
| | | |
|---|---|---|
| 00842019 | Level 1 Book/Audio | $9.99 |
| 00298773 | Level 2 Book/Audio | $9.95 |
| 00842041 | Songbook Book/Audio | $12.95 |
| 00699545 | Beginner's – Level 1 Book/Audio & DVD | $19.95 |
| 00702415 | Worship Songbook Book/Audio | $12.99 |
| 00703707 | Complete Kit | $22.99 |

## Play Recorder Today!
| | | |
|---|---|---|
| 00700919 | Level 1 Book/Audio | $7.99 |
| 00119830 | Complete Kit | $19.99 |

## Sing Today!
| | | |
|---|---|---|
| 00699761 | Level 1 Book/Audio | $10.99 |

## Play Trombone Today!
| | | |
|---|---|---|
| 00699917 | Level 1 Book/Audio | $12.99 |
| 00320508 | DVD | $14.95 |

## Play Trumpet Today!
| | | |
|---|---|---|
| 00842052 | Level 1 Book/Audio | $9.99 |
| 00842053 | Level 2 Book/Audio | $9.95 |
| 00320357 | DVD | $14.95 |
| 00842054 | Songbook Book/Audio | $12.95 |
| 00699556 | Beginner's – Level 1 Book/Audio & DVD | $19.95 |

## Play Ukulele Today!
| | | |
|---|---|---|
| 00699638 | Level 1 Book/Audio | $10.99 |
| 00699655 | Play Today Plus Book/Audio | $9.99 |
| 00320985 | DVD | $14.99 |
| 00701872 | Beginner's – Level 1 Book/Audio & DVD | $19.95 |
| 00650743 | Book/Audio/DVD with Ukulele | $39.99 |
| 00701002 | Level 2 Book/Audio | $9.99 |
| 00702484 | Level 2 Songbook Book/Audio | $12.99 |
| 00703290 | Starter | $24.99 |

## Play Viola Today!
| | | |
|---|---|---|
| 00142679 | Level 1 Book/Audio | $9.99 |

## Play Violin Today!
| | | |
|---|---|---|
| 00699748 | Level 1 Book/Audio | $9.99 |
| 00701320 | Level 2 Book/Audio | $9.99 |
| 00321076 | DVD | $14.99 |
| 00701700 | Songbook Book/Audio | $12.99 |
| 00701876 | Beginner's – Level 1 Book/Audio & DVD | $19.95 |

**www.halleonard.com**

# FIRST 50

You've been taking lessons, you've got a few chords under your belt, and you're ready to buy a songbook. Now what?
Hal Leonard has the answers in its *First 50* series.

These books contain easy to intermediate arrangements with lyrics for must-know songs.
Each arrangement is simple and streamlined, yet still captures the essence of the tune.

**First 50 Acoustic Songs You Should Play on Piano**
00293416 Easy Piano.........................$16.99

**First 50 Baroque Pieces You Should Play on Piano**
00291453 Easy Piano.........................$14.99

**First 50 Songs by the Beatles You Should Play on the Piano**
00172236 Easy Piano.......................$19.99

**First 50 Broadway Songs You Should Play on the Piano**
00150167 Easy Piano.........................$14.99

**First 50 Christmas Carols You Should Play on the Piano**
00147216 Easy Piano.........................$14.99

**First 50 Christmas Songs You Should Play on the Piano**
00172041 Easy Piano.........................$14.99

**First 50 Classic Rock Songs You Should Play on Piano**
00195619 Easy Piano.........................$16.99

**First 50 Classical Pieces You Should Play on the Piano**
00131436 Easy Piano Solo................$14.99

**First 50 Country Songs You Should Play on the Piano**
00150166 Easy Piano.........................$14.99

**First 50 Disney Songs You Should Play on the Piano**
00274938 Easy Piano.........................$16.99

**First 50 Early Rock Songs You Should Play on the Piano**
00160570 Easy Piano.........................$14.99

**First 50 Folk Songs You Should Play on the Piano**
00235867 Easy Piano.........................$14.99

**First 50 4-Chord Songs You Should Play on the Piano**
00249562 Easy Piano.........................$16.99

**First 50 Gospel Songs You Should Play on Piano**
00282526 Easy Piano.........................$14.99

**First 50 Hymns You Should Play on Piano**
00275199 Easy Piano.........................$14.99

**First 50 Jazz Standards You Should Play on Piano**
00196269 Easy Piano.........................$14.99

**First 50 Kids' Songs You Should Play on Piano**
00196071 Easy Piano.........................$14.99

**First 50 Latin Songs You Should Play on the Piano**
00248747 Easy Piano.........................$16.99

**First 50 Movie Songs You Should Play on the Piano**
00150165 Easy Piano.........................$16.99

**First 50 Movie Themes You Should Play on Piano**
00278368 Easy Piano.........................$16.99

**First 50 Songs You Should Play on the Organ**
00288203 .........................$19.99

**First 50 Piano Duets You Should Play**
00276571 1 Piano, 4 Hands...............$19.99

**First 50 Pop Ballads You Should Play on the Piano**
00248987 Easy Piano.........................$16.99

**First 50 Pop Hits You Should Play on the Piano**
00234374 Easy Piano.........................$16.99

**First 50 Popular Songs You Should Play on the Piano**
00131140 Easy Piano.........................$16.99

**First 50 R&B Songs You Should Play on Piano**
00196028 Easy Piano.........................$14.99

**First 50 3-Chord Songs You Should Play on Piano**
00249666 Easy Piano.........................$16.99

**First 50 Worship Songs You Should Play on Piano**
00287138 Easy Piano.........................$16.99

HAL•LEONARD®

**www.halleonard.com**

Prices, content and availability subject to change without notice.

# THE NEW DECADE SERIES
## EASY PIANO EDITIONS

The New Decade series books contain 80–100 iconic songs from each decade creating a complete historical library of popular music. These easy piano editions feature straightforward piano arrangements with lyrics.

**SONGS OF THE 1920s**

Among My Souvenirs • April Showers • Button up Your Overcoat • Bye Bye Blackbird • California, Here I Come • I'll See You in My Dreams • It Had to Be You • Let a Smile Be Your Umbrella • Look for the Silver Lining • Mack the Knife • Makin' Whoopee! • The Man I Love • My Blue Heaven • Puttin' on the Ritz • St. Louis Blues • Side by Side • Sleepy Time Gal • Stardust • Swanee • Yes Sir, That's My Baby • and more.
00282474.............................$24.99

**SONGS OF THE 1930s**

As Time Goes By • Blue Moon • Body and Soul • Embraceable You • Georgia on My Mind • The Glory of Love • I Don't Know Why (I Just Do) • I Got Rhythm • I'll Be Seeing You • In the Mood • The Lady Is a Tramp • Love Is Here to Stay • Mood Indigo • My Funny Valentine • The Nearness of You • Over the Rainbow • Sing, Sing, Sing • Summertime • The Very Thought of You • The Way You Look Tonight • and more.
00282475..........................$24.99

**SONGS OF THE 1940s**

Ac-cent-tchu-ate the Positive • Bésame Mucho (Kiss Me Much) • Boogie Woogie Bugle Boy • Don't Get Around Much Anymore • How High the Moon • I Get a Kick Out of You • It Might As Well Be Spring • Moonlight in Vermont • A Nightingale Sang in Berkeley Square • Route 66 • Sentimental Journey • Time After Time • When You Wish upon a Star • You'd Be So Nice to Come Home To • Zip-A-Dee-Doo-Dah • and more.
00282476.........................$24.99

**SONGS OF THE 1950s**

All I Have to Do Is Dream • Bye Bye Love • Chantilly Lace • Don't Be Cruel • Earth Angel • Fever • Great Balls of Fire • Hound Dog • I Walk the Line • It's So Easy • Kansas City • Lonely Teardrops • Mister Sandman • Only You (And You Alone) • Peter Gunn • Rock Around the Clock • Shout • Sixteen Tons • Tequila • Unchained Melody • Volare • Why Do Fools Fall in Love • Yakety Yak • Your Cheatin' Heart • and more.
00282477.............................$24.99

**SONGS OF THE 1960s**

Aquarius • Blowin' in the Wind • Do Wah Diddy Diddy • Downtown • God Only Knows • Good Vibrations • Happy Together • A Hard Day's Night • I Saw Her Standing There • I'm a Believer • King of the Road • Leaving on a Jet Plane • The Letter • The Loco-Motion • Louie, Louie • Mr. Tambourine Man • Monday, Monday • Oh, Pretty Woman • Proud Mary • (Sittin' On) the Dock of the Bay • The Sound of Silence • The Twist • Wichita Lineman • Wild Thing • and more.
00282478.............................$24.99

**SONGS OF THE 1970s**

ABC • American Pie • Bridge over Troubled Water • (They Long to Be) Close to You • Dancing Queen • Free Bird • Goodbye Yellow Brick Road • How Deep Is Your Love • I Shot the Sheriff • I Will Survive • Imagine • Killing Me Softly with His Song • Layla • Lean on Me • Maybe I'm Amazed • Piano Man • Reeling in the Years • Smoke on the Water • Stairway to Heaven • Stayin' Alive • Sweet Home Alabama • Time in a Bottle • Walk This Way • We Will Rock You • Y.M.C.A. • and more.
00282479..........................$24.99

**SONGS OF THE 1980s**

Another Brick in the Wall • Billie Jean • Chariots of Fire • Don't Stop Believin' • Endless Love • Eye of the Tiger • Flashdance... What a Feeling • How Will I Know • I Love Rock 'N Roll • Jump • Missing You • Nothing's Gonna Stop Us Now • Pour Some Sugar on Me • Right Here Waiting • Sweet Child O' Mine • Take on Me • Time After Time • Up Where We Belong • What's Love Got to Do with It • With or Without You • and more.
00282480.............................$24.99

**SONGS OF THE 1990s**

Always Be My Baby • As Long As You Love Me • Black Velvet • Can You Feel the Love Tonight • Dreams • Fields of Gold • Friends in Low Places • Good Riddance (Time of Your Life) • How Am I Supposed to Live Without You • I Need to Know • I'm the Only One • Ironic • Livin' La Vida Loca • Losing My Religion • More Than Words • Only Wanna Be with You • Smells like Teen Spirit • Smooth • Tears in Heaven • Under the Bridge • You're Still the One • and more.
00282481.............................$24.99

**SONGS OF THE 2000s**

Beautiful • Before He Cheats • Bye Bye Bye • Chasing Pavements • Don't Know Why • Drive • Fallin' • Hey There Delilah • I Gotta Feeling • I'm Yours • Just Dance • Love Story • Mercy • Only Time • The Reason • Rehab • This Love • A Thousand Miles • Umbrella • Viva La Vida • Waiting on the World to Change • With Arms Wide Open • You Raise Me Up • and more.
00282482.............................$24.99

**SONGS OF THE 2010s**

All About That Bass • Bad Romance • Brave • Call Me Maybe • Cups (When I'm Gone) • Feel It Still • Get Lucky • Happy • Havana • Hey, Soul Sister • I Will Wait • Just Give Me a Reason • Let It Go • Mean • Moves like Jagger • Need You Now • Radioactive • Rolling in the Deep • Shake It Off • Stay with Me • Thinking Out Loud • Uptown Funk • We Are Young • and more.
00282483.............................$24.99

**HAL•LEONARD®**
www.halleonard.com

*Prices, contents, and availability subject to change without notice.*